Fire and Ice

For Colin,

who loves cold northern

landscapes too.

Darby Creek
A division of Lerner Publishing Group, Inc.
241 First Avenue North
Minneapolis, MN 55401 USA

For reading levels and more information, look up this title at
www.lernerbooks.com.

Main body text set in Sabon LT Std 13/19.
Typeface provided by Adobe Systems.

Library of Congress Cataloging-in-Publication Data

Cataloging-in-Publication Data for *Fire and Ice* is on file at the Library of
Congress.
ISBN 978-1-5124-1320-5 (lib. bdg.)
ISBN 978-1-5124-1345-8 (pbk.)
ISBN 978-1-5124-1346-5 (EB pdf)

Manufactured in the United States of America
1-39779-21317-2/24/2016

WORLD of STORIES

Fire and Ice

STORIES OF WINTER FROM AROUND THE WORLD

LARI DON

Illustrated by
Francesca Greenwood

darbycreek
MINNEAPOLIS

Contents

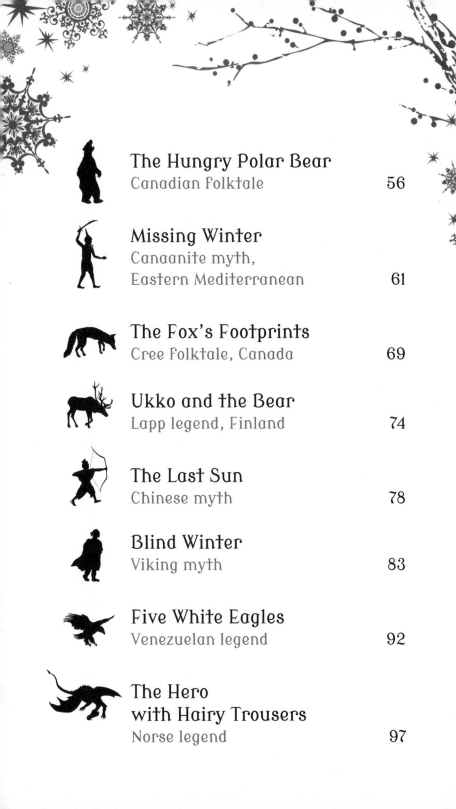

The Seeds of Winter
Greek myth

When the gods were young, there was no winter.

There was no winter, no spring, no summer, and no autumn. Just warmth and growth, with fruit heavy in the trees and grain tall in the fields. Every month brought a new crop to harvest and everyone ate well.

The goddess Demeter was always busy because it was her job to encourage all the plants to grow, but she was happy too.

Demeter had a daughter she loved very

much: Persephone, whose father was the chief god, Zeus. So, with her beloved plants and her beloved child both growing healthy and strong, Demeter was a glowing, generous presence on Earth.

Persephone grew into a beautiful young woman: tall, slim, and golden, like the wheat in her mother's fields.

One sunny day, Persephone was picnicking with her friends at the edge of a field. They had eaten so much of the earth's goodness—apple pies, cucumber sandwiches, honey cakes—that all her friends were full and sleepy.

But Persephone noticed something in the center of the field. A plant she had never seen before, dark and glittering in the distance.

She asked her friends if they would come with her to examine the plant, but they yawned and said they would join her later.

So Persephone walked on her own toward the plant. As she

got closer, she could see it was covered with black flowers. As she got closer still, she could see silver tips on each black petal. She knew all of her mother's plants, but she had never seen flowers so gloriously dark and sharp.

There were nine blossoms and Persephone decided it wouldn't harm the plant if she picked just one of them to show her mother.

So Persephone reached out to pluck the nearest flower.

But her fingers stuck to the stem. She couldn't break the stem, and she couldn't pull her hand away.

The flower trembled. The whole plant shivered. Then the plant jerked and started to sink into the ground, as if something was pulling on the roots.

Persephone yelled for help, but her friends were asleep.

The plant was dragged down into the crumbling earth and Persephone was dragged down after it.

And she landed in the underworld.

She landed at the feet of Hades, the god

of the underworld, the king of the dead.

Hades had heard of Persephone's golden beauty and he wanted her to brighten his dark land. So he had grown the black flowers to tempt her and he had pulled on the roots to steal her away.

"Will you be my queen?" he asked.

Hades offered Persephone the black blossoms as a wedding bouquet and he offered her a table of fragrant food as a wedding feast.

Persephone looked around at the dark glories and riches of the underworld. She heard the whispered histories and knowledge of the dead. She smiled at Hades and she accepted the flowers, but she didn't eat any of the feast because she suspected eating the food of the underworld could trap her there forever.

Up above, Demeter was starting to panic. Persephone hadn't come home after the picnic, and although Demeter had no idea where her daughter was, she was afraid someone had taken her.

So she rushed to Olympus and demanded to see Zeus.

"Where is our daughter?" she sobbed.

The most powerful of the gods frowned, then shrugged. He had a lot of children and it was hard to keep track of them all.

But Demeter's grief was growing louder and Zeus was fond of Persephone, so he sent Hermes, the messenger of the gods, to investigate. Hermes returned with rumors of a new queen in the underworld, with hair more golden than a crown.

"That's her!" cried Demeter. "That's Persephone! Bring her back! Please, Zeus, bring our girl back!"

So Zeus sent Hermes down to the underworld with instructions to ask Hades politely to give the girl back to her mother.

But Hades refused. "She's happy here, aren't you, dear? And she makes me happy. What would she do back at her mother's, anyway? Weed the garden and thin out the carrots? She's wasted there. Tell Zeus I'm keeping her here."

Hermes took that message back to Zeus, who shrugged and said there was nothing he could do.

Demeter wailed and screamed and stomped around the marble halls of Olympus. Then she calmed down and said in a quiet voice, "If you are going to do nothing, then I will do nothing too. I will do nothing at all."

And she did indeed do nothing. Demeter refused to help the plants and grass and crops grow.

She sat in a corner, weeping and muttering and refusing to do anything. While she was in such a dark mood, nothing could grow. No grass, no flowers, no fruit, no crops. Nothing grew.

When the grass stopped growing, the animals became thin and hungry.

When the crops failed, the people were soon thin and hungry as well.

Eventually the people had so little food, they stopped sending up offerings to the gods.

The gods became hungry too.

Zeus looked around at the barren hungry world and decided that he'd better get Persephone back after all.

So he summoned Hermes. "Return to the underworld and demand that Hades hand over Persephone, and make that demand in the name of the highest god, in the name of Zeus, the god of thunder . . ."

Before Hermes started on his journey to the underworld, Hades and Persephone already knew he was coming. When Zeus thundered, everyone heard, so everyone knew what Hermes' mission was.

Hades turned to Persephone as they sat on their ivory thrones and held out a handful of blood-red seeds. "You must be hungry, my dear. Please accept these seeds."

Persephone knew it was time to make a choice.

She could eat the twelve blood-red seeds and stay forever in the underworld, with all the power of the queen of the dead.

Or she could refuse to eat the twelve blood-red seeds and return to the light, to be her mother's daughter forever.

Persephone took the twelve seeds from Hades' white hand.

As she raised the seeds to her lips, Hermes arrived on his feathered feet and announced, "Zeus the thunderer demands the return of his daughter."

"It's too late," smiled Hades. "She has already eaten the food of the underworld. She must stay here forever."

"Not forever," said Persephone.

She opened her fingers and showed eight blood-red seeds still glowing in the palm of her hand.

"I only ate four of the twelve seeds. So I will stay with you for four months of the year, and I will return to the sunlight and my mother's fields for the rest of the year."

So now the gods are older, and we have winter.

We have winter for the four months of the year that Persephone is in the underworld, when Demeter grieves for her daughter and refuses to let the plants grow.

Then comes spring, when Persephone returns and Demeter's joy brings life and growth.

Then summer, when everyone is settled into contented happiness.

Then autumn, when Demeter sinks slowly into sadness as she remembers her daughter must leave again.

And then winter returns, when Demeter grieves once more and no plants grow anywhere.

No plants except the glittering black flowers that Persephone grows in the underworld.

The Snow Bear
and the Trolls
Norwegian Folktale

The King of Denmark wanted a snow bear. Other kings owned lions and tigers and giraffes and unicorns, so he wanted a big, fancy pet too. He offered a reward to the first man to bring a snow bear to his palace.

Lars was a farmboy who had always wanted to see the king's palace. So he traveled to Finnmark, in the far north of Norway, and

he tracked a great, white snow bear. He laid a
trap, baited it with seal meat, then he caught
the bear in his net and locked an iron chain
around her neck.

He said, "Come on, my beautiful white
bear. I will take you to the King of Denmark
and you will wear gold chains around your
neck and be admired and fed all sorts of good
food. Follow me to Copenhagen to live a life
of gold and warmth and comfort."

The snow bear looked around at the hard,
cold, silver ice, then she sat down on her
bottom and refused to move.

Lars pulled on her iron chain and told
her all about the wonders of the palace, the
generosity of the king, and the splendors of
the city. None of which he had seen, all of
which he had dreamed about.

But she sat firmly on her large, white bottom
and wouldn't move. And a snow bear is very
heavy if she doesn't want to move.

Lars kept tugging, chatting cheerfully about
the king's palace and dangling raw meat in
front of her.

Eventually the snow bear shrugged, stood, and followed Lars.

And they walked together over the ice, then through forests, to the mountains and water of the lands where it is not winter all year round. But as they walked south, it became winter there too, as if the bear had brought the snow with her.

They walked through the frosty mountains, Lars hunting for food for them both.

When they reached the farmlands at the edge of the mountains, a blizzard began. The cold, howling storm didn't bother the bear at all, but Lars was getting tired, his boots were wearing thin, and it was taking longer than he thought to reach the king's palace.

Through the swirls of snow, he saw the lights of a farmhouse. He and the snow bear walked to the door, pushing against the wind and snow, and Lars knocked.

A farmer and his daughter opened the door.

"Can we shelter with you tonight, please?" asked Lars.

The farmer shook his head. "I'm sorry.

Even though this is Christmas Eve, we can't welcome guests."

Lars said, "Are you worried about the bear? She'll be fine. She's on her way to be the king's snow bear, and she's been as gentle as a kitten all the way here."

The bear smiled, showing all her teeth. The farmer backed away, but his daughter smiled at the bear and at Lars.

"No," said the daughter, "it's not the bear. It's the trolls. It's Christmas Day tomorrow and the trolls will come and eat our Christmas feast. They break in every year, wreck our furniture, rip our curtains, and attack anyone who stays in the house. So we leave them our feast to distract them from destroying the house completely, and we hide in the mountains until they've gone. You can come with us to the mountains, if you like."

Lars sighed. "I've just walked through the mountains. I don't want to go back. Anyway, I'm not scared of trolls and neither is this bear. We'll stay here and show them what happens to trolls who ruin a family's Christmas."

So the farmer and his daughter went to their freezing cold hiding place, leaving Lars and the bear in the house, with a huge Christmas feast piled on the kitchen table.

The travelers were both tired, so Lars curled up in a corner and the snow bear curled up under the table and they went to sleep.

Then the clock on the mantelpiece ticked around to midnight and the trolls arrived. Eight huge, green-skinned, warty-nosed, hairy-handed, pot-bellied trolls with incredibly stinky feet crashed through the door. Lars slid deeper into the shadows, more scared of trolls than he'd admitted.

The trolls slumped down around the table, they slobbered and snottered all over the food, they held burping contests and sang rude songs, and they prodded each other with cutlery and bones.

Then the wartiest troll looked under the table. "Oi! Look! A pretty white cat! I wonder what roast cat tastes like?" The troll prodded at the white animal with a long spoon.

The bear opened one eye.

The troll prodded her again.

The bear stood.

As she stood, the table and the feast rose up on her shoulders. When she straightened her spine, the table and the feast slid down her fur and crashed onto the floor.

The bear reached her full, huge height and roared.

She stretched and broke the thin iron chain that Lars had put around her neck. She swiped her heavy paws in a circle, knocking all the trolls to the floor.

She roared again, giving the trolls a close-up view of her long, sharp teeth.

The trolls shrieked and ran out of the door, whimpering about scary cats and leaving nothing behind but their stink.

Then the bear lay back down to sleep and Lars tidied up the mess.

When the farmer and his daughter returned on Christmas morning, Lars said he had an idea to stop the trolls coming back. As he explained, the farmer's daughter smiled at him again. And Lars decided he wasn't interested in seeing the king's palace after all.

So Lars stayed at the farm and married the farmer's daughter.

And the snow bear? She had never been interested in gold chains and warm comfort, so she waved goodbye to Lars and followed her own trail back to her icy, silver home.

Next Christmas Eve, Lars put a sign on the farmhouse door:

Our white cat has just had kittens.

Free to good homes in the spring.

So the trolls went somewhere else for their Christmas feast.

I hope it wasn't your house . . .

The Prince of Wolves
Tsimshian Folktale, Canada

It was the darkest month of winter; food was scarce and the Tsimshian people were huddling together to keep warm and cheerful. But the wind was shrieking and howling around the village, which made the children cry and the old folk shiver.

"That's not just the wind," said a boy.

"Yes it is," said his grandfather.

"No, there's another howl in there. Not the

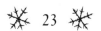

angry wind, but something sadder. Something scared. Something in pain."

Everyone listened. There wasn't much to do but listen to the wind, apart from shiver and rub their empty bellies. The wind howled again. But now they could hear something else: a thread of another howl, just beyond the edge of the wild wind.

"It's a wolf!" said the boy. "It's a wolf howling."

The people shivered even more. They were cold and weak and didn't want to worry about a pack of hungry wolves circling the village.

"But it's only one wolf," said the boy. "And it sounds scared. It sounds like it needs help."

The wolf howled again, the sound suddenly clearer during a lull in the wind.

The boy stood. "I'm going to help the wolf."

"No!" said his grandmother. "You can't help a wolf because you can't trust a wolf."

But the boy heard the lonely howl again and left the village. He walked into the forest,

ignoring the swirling of the wind and snow, following the sound of the sad howls. Soon he could hear whines too.

Then he saw the wolf. A big gray wolf, slumped in the middle of a clearing, with red-rimmed eyes and heaving ribs. His howls were as loud as a storm now the boy was so close, but his whines were soft and gasping.

The boy looked at the wolf. The wolf looked at the boy.

"Do you need help?" asked the boy.

The wolf whined.

The boy walked up to the wolf.

The wolf opened his long, fanged jaws and the boy saw a spike of bone sticking out of the back of the wolf's swollen throat.

The boy looked into the wolf's yellow eyes, then put his right hand carefully into the wolf's mouth and pulled out the jagged bone.

The wolf collapsed onto the ground, drops of his blood spotting the snow.

The boy nodded to the wolf and turned to go. At least the whining and howling had stopped.

But as he walked away, the boy was knocked to the ground.

He rolled over in a panic.

The wolf was standing over him, teeth bared in a snarl.

You can't trust a wolf, thought the boy.

Then the wolf lowered his furry, gray head and rubbed it against the boy's chest. The wolf looked up again, teeth still bared. But perhaps, thought the boy, it was a smile, not a snarl.

The boy stood, said farewell to the wolf, and walked back to the village to join his hungry huddled family.

The next day, over the constant howl of the wind, he heard another howl close by. Then he saw the big, gray wolf trotting around the village.

So the boy went out to meet the wolf. The wolf led him into the forest to a newly slain deer, which the boy

dragged back to the village for his people to roast and eat.

The next day, the wolf called him again. But this time the wolf didn't show the boy a dead deer. This time, the wolf showed the boy how to hunt. He showed the boy how wolves hunt: how they track their prey, how the wolf pack works together, how they move silently and wait for the right moment.

So the boy learned to hunt like a wolf, and every day that winter he brought fresh meat back to his village. Then, when everyone was strong enough, the boy taught the rest of the Tsimshian people the secrets of the wolf hunt.

The people were so grateful for the good food the boy brought during the winter and the new hunting skills the boy taught them that when he grew to be a man they gave him a new name.

They called him the Prince of Wolves.

And though he was an important and powerful man in their culture, the Prince of Wolves still liked to spend most of his days in the forest. Hunting with a big, gray wolf.

The Ibis Brings Spring
Yamana myth, Tierra del Fuego

The Yamana people of Tierra del Fuego live in the rocky lands at the tip of South America, closer to the South Pole than any other towns and villages on Earth.

Every year, they know winter is ending and spring is on its way when they see the ibis woman, Lexuwa, with her long, curved beak and her long, red legs, fly over their villages.

One year, when an old man sitting at the door of his hut saw the ibis flying toward his village, he was so happy that he stood and yelled, "Look! Here comes Lexuwa the ibis! Winter is over! Spring is here!"

The villagers ran out of their huts. Everyone shouted and cheered. The children bounced up and down, squealing and shrieking. They all pointed their fingers at the ibis and shouted, "Look, the ibis! The ibis brings spring!"

But Lexuwa the ibis woman was shy, and she didn't like people looking at her or shouting about her or pointing at her.

So she turned around and flew away, taking spring with her.

And winter stayed. Winter got deeper and colder. The snow kept falling; the glaciers in the valleys grew thicker and higher. It was impossible to get canoes out to sea, everyone's winter food stocks ran out, and sometimes the blizzards were so fierce people couldn't leave their huts to collect firewood.

Many people froze, many people starved, and the people who survived longed for spring.

But they knew they could not shout to the ibis to ask her to bring spring because that would drive her further away. So after many long months of a winter with the strength to last forever, they realized what they must do.

They *whispered* their request to the ibis.

They whispered, gently and respectfully, into the cold air. "Beautiful ibis, beautiful Lexuwa, please end this long heavy winter. Please bring spring and we will never offend you again."

So the ibis brought spring. She flew back over the village and as she flew over, winter ended and spring began.

But the people's troubles were not over.

The long winter had trapped massive quantities of water in the snow and glaciers. So when the warm spring sun melted the ice, it caused the great flood, which is remembered in many stories around the world.

The floodwaters rose so high that the Yamana retreated to the mountain tops, waiting for the water level to fall before they

could return to the coast and rebuild their
huts.

Once the floodwaters had gone, the seasons
settled back into their rhythm.

Now, when the people see the ibis woman
approach, they don't shout and point. They
stay still and quiet. They send the children
into the huts and they shush the little ones,
so no one makes a noise and no one offends
the ibis.

Because they hope the ibis will always bring
spring, rather than bring another long winter
and another great flood.

The Hag of Winter
Scottish myth

Winter made the land.

In ancient times the winter hag, the Cailleach, carried a basket of stones and rocks on her back and waded through the sea. When she reached the right place, she tipped the basket over her head so the rocks and stones poured out into the sea.

The stones that bounced away became the islands scattered down the west coast of

Scotland, and the rocks that landed in a pile became the mainland of Scotland.

The Cailleach smashed the pile of rocks together to make one land with her great, heavy mallet. Her hammer crushed the rocks together but also froze them hard, because everything the winter hag's mallet touched became ice cold, barren, and lifeless.

Then the Cailleach ruled the land. Her reign of dark and ice lasted for many cold years. She hoped it would last forever.

Only one person could end her reign: her son, Angus Og.

Angus, with his red-gold hair, was born to be the god of summer. So he could end the reign of winter. But Angus could only become god of summer and end the endless winter if he married a girl called Brid, the girl who was born to be spring.

When the Cailleach discovered this, she banished her son, then she kidnapped Brid and held her prisoner in a hollow mountain.

So while Angus strode up and down Scotland searching for his mother's hiding

place, the Cailleach sat on her ice-cold throne in the center of the mountain, surrounded by her storm hags, with her prisoner in a small stone cell.

But hiding in a hollow mountain becomes boring after a while, so the Cailleach decided to entertain herself by teasing and tormenting Brid. She knew that despair is a terrible thing but that a glimmer of impossible hope is even worse.

She dragged Brid from her cell and said, "I will never let you go, unless you can wash *this* pure white in the running water of the creek outside."

She threw a filthy, crusty, gray-brown sheepskin at Brid's feet.

So every day Brid was allowed out to crouch by the cold creek flowing down the side of the hollow mountain and wash the fleece in the ice-rimmed water.

She couldn't run away because she was guarded by the storm hags. A dozen huge, bitter old women, with blue faces, tusks for teeth, matted white hair, and one gray eye

each sat near the creek on their shaggy goats as Brid scrubbed and rubbed.

Every day while Brid washed the fleece, she wondered how she could escape or let Angus know where she was hidden.

For one hundred days she scrubbed the fleece, until her hands were red raw with the cold water, her nails were splintered, and her knuckles were bleeding.

Each day the water in the creek ran away dark and filthy from the fleece. Each night she had to show the filthy fleece to the Cailleach, who taunted Brid about her failure to wash it clean.

Then, after one hundred days, the water began to run clear. Brid had rinsed all the dirt out of the fleece but the wool was still brown.

However, Brid kept washing the fleece every day because she knew she had more chance to escape, or to signal Angus, on the mountainside than inside her stone cell. So she kept scrubbing and rubbing at the brown fleece, her hands cold and sore and raw.

Then one day, she noticed a line of tiny

flowers pushing up through the hard cold ground by the side of the creek.

Brid realized that Angus must have walked this way searching for her.

Because although Angus Og was not yet the god of summer, he held all the warmth of future summers inside him. So as he walked on the frozen ground, the warmth of his tread softened the earth enough for plants to grow for a little while.

Brid didn't say anything. She just kept scrubbing until one short moment when none of the storm hags were looking straight at her. She quickly plucked a flower and hid it in her cloak.

That evening when she was taken before the Cailleach to show the fleece, the winter hag laughed down at Brid from the icy throne. "You've still not washed it pure white, you useless girl!"

Brid said quietly, "Of course I haven't washed it pure white. However clean it is, this fleece will never be white because it came from a *brown* sheep, you cold, cruel old woman.

And I know this now because I have seen pure white."

The Cailleach shrugged. "You have seen the pure white of my snow and ice."

Brid shook her head. "No, the white I have seen is purer and clearer and brighter than that. The purest, most beautiful white of all is the white of the first flower at the end of winter."

And Brid pulled from her cloak . . .

A snowdrop.

As soon as she saw the tiny flower, the Cailleach screamed a scream of rage and fear that echoed around the hollow mountain then boomed across the whole of Scotland. Just as Brid had planned.

Angus heard the scream; he recognized his mother's voice and he followed the sound to the mountain.

Faster than his mother could think or the storm hags could move, Angus burst into the hollow mountain, grabbed Brid's hand, and the two of them ran.

They ran as far and as fast as they could.

The Cailleach knew that if Brid and Angus, spring and summer, stayed together, then winter would be over. So she sent her storm hags after them to separate them or kill them.

The storm hags chased Brid and Angus around and across Scotland.

Every time they were trapped or ambushed, Brid and Angus stood back to back and fought together.

The storm hags attacked with their weapons of biting cold and slicing wind.

Brid and Angus fought back with their own weapons: Angus with his sword, red-gold and bright like his hair; Brid with the fleece she had washed so often, long and supple.

He stabbed and slashed and parried with blows of the sword. She blinded the one-eyed hags and tripped the goats with flicks of the fleece.

They fought every day for weeks. On the days when Brid and Angus were winning, the weather was warm and bright and clear, and plants began to grow. On the days the storm

hags were winning, the weather was cold and dark and frosty, and new growth was nipped in the bud.

The battle went on for weeks, up and down the whole land. But finally Brid and Angus prevailed. At last, all the storm hags were dead and their goats were limping away.

Spring and summer stood together, triumphant.

So the Cailleach came out of her mountain.

She stomped toward them, her massive mallet striking the ground with every step. The mallet froze and killed everything it touched. All the new plants, all the new growth, all the new hope.

The Cailleach was the coldest, the strongest, the hardest, the most destructive being on this Earth. Nothing Brid or Angus could do would stop her, no weapon they could hold would defeat her.

The Cailleach stomped closer and closer, destroying everything before her with crashing blows of her mallet.

Angus called out to the sun, because he

knew the sun longed for summer. He called for help to defeat his mother.

So the sun forged a spear from boiling air and burning fire and aimed the white-hot weapon at the Cailleach's back as she marched toward Brid and Angus.

But the Cailleach ducked out of the way and the sun's spear missed her, gouging a line right across Scotland as it fell to Earth.

Though the Cailleach dodged the burning blade, the pure heat of the spear passed so close to her that it melted her icy core of strength. The Cailleach collapsed to the ground, exhausted after her long reign.

She dropped her mallet under a holly bush—which is why nothing grows under a holly bush, not even in the most fertile spring or the warmest summer—and she crawled away to one of the stony islands she had dropped from her basket.

The winter hag lay on the island, barely breathing, unable to wake. While she slept, Brid and Angus brought life to the world. Life and hope and growth and warmth and color.

That is why every year spring weather veers between days of bright clear warmth and days of dark cold frost. Because spring is a battle between winter and summer. A battle that summer always wins.

But summer doesn't win for long.

Every autumn, the Cailleach wakes up. And she reaches for her mallet . . .

The Spiders' Christmas
Ukrainian Folktale

It was Christmas Eve and the children were cleaning the house for Santa.

"But he comes down the *chimney*!" said the smallest girl. "He'll be covered in soot. He won't care if our house is dusty or not. He won't even notice."

"Yes he will," said their mother. "I want our house to be the cleanest, tidiest, shiniest house in the whole village. So pick up those socks!"

The children tidied, dusted, polished, and mopped all day.

"I don't want to see any dust or dirt, any cobwebs or fluff," said their mother cheerfully.

"Christmas is hard work," the smallest boy muttered.

"Cobwebs!" called out their mother. "I see cobwebs on the ceiling."

So the biggest girl climbed the ladder and the biggest boy held it steady. She flicked with a feather duster until the cobwebs vanished.

A family of spiders were hiding in the darkest corner of the ceiling. As the dust and cobwebs were swept out of the house, the littlest spider whispered, "Where will we live now? If those huge people flick all our webs away, where will we live?"

The mother spider said, "Don't worry. This big clean only lasts one day and we can weave more webs once their winter festival is over. But watch what happens next."

The little spiders watched as the children's father arrived with a tall, green, sharp-needled

tree. The smell of the outdoors followed the tree into the house.

The children clapped and cheered and got in the way while their father put the tree in a bucket and jammed stones around the trunk to keep it upright.

Then the biggest boy held the ladder again, and the little spiders crept deeper into the corner. "It's fine," said their mother. "They're not coming up here again. Look."

The children were hanging glass globes, gingerbread men, and little metal drums from the branches of the great green tree. They put a bright star, gleaming like the rest of the house, on the very top of the tree.

Then the whole family stood in a circle around the tree and sang lots of happy songs. Finally, they all went upstairs to bed.

"Hurry up," said the children's mother, "you want to be asleep before Santa comes down the chimney."

The spiders gazed at the tree.

"It's magic," said the littlest spider. "It's like we have a forest in our house!"

"Go to sleep," said the mother spider. "We'll need lots of energy to weave more webs."

But while she fell asleep, the little spiders stayed awake, looking at the tree.

"Let's go closer," said the biggest baby spider.

They swung down on their spider silk, from the rafters to the top of the tree.

Then the little spiders played on the tree.

They waved at their reflections in the glass globes, played marching tunes on the tiny drums with all their feet, and danced around the gingerbread men. They leaped from branch to branch, singing the songs they had heard the family sing, and played hide and seek behind the dark green needles. They climbed up to the shiny star, daring each other to perch on the highest point. Then they challenged each other to a rappelling race from the star to the bucket.

As they dared and danced and raced and played, the little

spiders left a maze of delicate spider silk all over the tree. Long lines of white, zigzagging around the tree, winding around the branches.

Then, suddenly, they heard a thump and a creak.

A big man in a red suit landed in front of the fireplace.

The baby spiders hid deep in the shadows of the tree, right against the trunk.

Santa Claus walked to the tree and looked at the pale threads chasing around it.

And he laughed.

He looked around the clean, gleaming, shining house and said, "Let's make it *all* shine!"

He touched the nearest thread of spider silk and it glowed silver. Santa nodded, then ran his gloved finger down another strand and all the spider silk around the tree gleamed like silver. The whole tree shone.

Then Santa bent down, peered between the branches, and winked at the little spiders.

Once he had filled all the stockings on the mantelpiece, he clambered back up the

chimney. The little spiders scampered back to the ceiling to snuggle up beside their mother.

The next morning, when the family came downstairs, they found their presents and they also found their tree covered in the very first tinsel.

Ever since that day, children in the Ukraine and Germany have decorated Christmas trees with strings of shining tinsel, but they also hide a little toy spider deep inside the branches.

Ice and Fire
Maori myth, New Zealand

The Maoris tell of their arrival in Aotearoa more than six hundred years ago, in a Great Fleet of canoes.

Skilled Polynesian navigators had known about the long, cloudy southern islands, which we also call New Zealand, for many generations. But it was not until food shortages and arguments made the tropical island Hawaiki uncomfortable that they built a Great Fleet of eight huge canoes to

journey to colder southern waters and settle Aotearoa.

Those who were staying on Hawaiki came to the beach to wave the Great Fleet off, and the young priest Ngatoro and his sister Kuiwai were at the front of the crowd. The captain of one of the canoes called Ngatoro over and asked him to come aboard for a moment to bless the boat with his powerful magic.

So Ngatoro climbed aboard and started to call down blessings on the canoe and its voyage.

But as Ngatoro stood in the middle of the boat, the captain shouted the order to set sail. He wanted to keep the priest on board to bless not just the boat and the journey but the new homeland too.

Ngatoro could have leaped overboard or halted the boat with storms and curses. But when he felt the canoe move on the waves and he smelled the open sea, he smiled. He was curious to see this new cold land. So he waved goodbye to Kuiwai and he allowed the captain to take him south.

When the Great Fleet landed after their long journey, Ngatoro was busy for days. Everyone wanted a priest's blessing: on their arrival, on their new home, on their source of fresh water, on their future.

When all the settlers were finally happy in their new homes, Ngatoro realized he had no home of his own. He had been so busy blessing everyone else's newly claimed land, he hadn't claimed his own land yet. Now it might be too late because all the land near the coast was taken.

He looked inland and saw a mountain topped with a smooth white cap. Ngatoro thought that if he climbed the mountain, he would be able to see for miles and any land he could see, he could name and claim for himself. So he began to climb the mountain.

As he climbed higher and higher, he gasped at the coldness of the air around him. Then he noticed that his sharp out-breaths were forming clouds in the air. It was a new magic, one he did not know, but it was a beautiful,

dancing magic. He laughed, blowing out puffs and streams of pale cloud.

Then he reached the white cap on the upper slopes of the mountain. It wasn't solid pale rock as he'd expected or even pure silver sand as he had seen on beaches. It was something more fragile: crisp and crunching under his feet, crushed into permanent footprints behind him and very cold on his toes.

He bent down and touched the white crust on the ground. It burned his fingers like fire, but when he picked up a handful of white, it crumbled, then melted into cold clear water on his skin.

Ngatoro continued up the mountain, determined to get to the top and see as far as he could.

He was shaking now, shivering like a half-drowned sailor or a child with fever. His teeth were clacking together and he was rubbing his hands to keep them warm. His shoulders were hunched against the cold and wind. His legs were aching from the steep climb and the unfamiliar crunching surface.

But finally Ngatoro reached the top of the mountain and looked around.

The land below was glorious. He saw forests and rivers and meadows. He named and claimed as much land as he thought one man could love, which was not even one tenth of what he saw.

Then he started to climb down. It wasn't easy because the cold white ground slipped away under his feet and he had to fight to keep his balance.

As he stumbled and slid down the mountain, he discovered where the white cold came from.

It came from the sky.

It started to fall in cold white flakes from the clouds in the sky, and it fluttered down to land on the ground and on his own head and shoulders.

Ngatoro laughed again. He was glad he had been tricked into coming on the canoe to find this new white magic.

He stopped and raised his hands to greet the flakes.

But then the wind grew stronger and the flakes fell faster. His shivering became more violent and the ground was harder to walk on. The wind grew even wilder and the flakes swirled around him so he couldn't see where he was going.

Ngatoro slipped and landed hard, his body flat on the ground. He was buried in the white cold, with the flakes landing on him and covering him. Suddenly he was so cold and so tired that he couldn't even shiver.

Ngatoro knew he was dying. He could feel the life start to leave his body.

So he called out for help. Not to the people on the coast below; they were too far away and had no power to help him.

He called to someone even further away, someone who had plenty of power.

He called to his sister Kuiwai, at home in Hawaiki.

And Kuiwai knew his pain. She felt his fear and sadness in her own heart. She felt the

burning cold on her own skin and she felt the deep cold in her own bones.

She knew she had to be quick if she was going to save her brother.

So Kuiwai grabbed a branch from the fire, a long sturdy branch with a blazing flame at the end. And she leaped into the sea.

Kuiwai used her power to keep the branch burning as she swam faster than lightning under the sea all the way to Aotearoa.

When she reached the north island, she didn't stop and she didn't come ashore. She just kept swimming under the land, faster than an arrow, toward the mountain where her brother lay with his last breaths billowing around his face.

Kuiwai forced her way under the land until she reached the mountain. Then she burst upward and out of the summit, ripping a hole in the mountain. She landed hard on the white ground with the branch still burning in her hand.

She ran to her brother so fast she didn't even leave footprints on the white land, she

wrapped her arms around him, and she used her warmth and the burning flame to coax the life back into his body.

And Ngatoro woke up.

Then brother and sister walked, arm in arm, down the mountain to make a home together in their new land.

And that is why Aotearoa is a land of both ice and fire. Because the path Kuiwai took under the land is now a line of hot springs and the hole where she burst out of the summit with her flaming torch is now a volcano.

Aotearoa is a land of fire as well as ice because a sister used all her power and speed to save her brother from his first ever blizzard.

The Hungry Polar Bear
Canadian Folktale

A father and his son were away from their village, fishing on the coast of the cold north. They couldn't reach home before darkness fell, so they settled down for the night. They built a wall of ice blocks by a hillside, then sheltered between the wall and the slope and built a fire to keep the small space warm.

The father held onto his harpoon and the boy clutched his knife in his hand, ready to

defend themselves and their catch from any other hunters who might want to make a meal of them.

But one hunter smelled the fire, the fish, and the people, and thought it smelled like his supper.

He was a big polar bear, white from his ears to his toes, but he was thin and hungry.

The polar bear crept to the wall of ice, looked over, and saw the father with his barbed harpoon and the boy with his sharp knife. The bear didn't want to attack them, in case they woke up fast enough to hurt him with those blades.

So he backed away and he thought for a long time, his thoughts interrupted occasionally by the chirping of a little brown bird on the hill.

Then the polar bear came up with a plan. If he put out the fire, then the man and the boy would freeze, and he could eat them and their fish without any danger from their weapons.

So the bear crept, as slowly and quietly as a bear on huge, white paws can creep, right up to the fire.

He patted the fire with his left paw.

It was hot! He jerked his paw back and shook it.

Then he patted the fire with his right paw.

It burned his paw! He jerked his paw back and shook it.

And he patted each little flame flat. Patting, and shaking and blowing on his sore paws to cool them down. He patted and patted with his paws until the flames were all gone, leaving only tiny glowing embers in the ashes.

Then the bear backed off to wait for the air to cool down and the father and son to freeze. Once they were frozen solid, he would be able to eat his meal in safety.

As the polar bear waited and the little bird on the hill watched, the father and son started to freeze. Icicles formed around their mouths and nostrils. Their breathing slowed and their hearts slowed.

But as the polar bear was deciding which one to eat first, the little brown bird fluttered over to the fire and started to flap his wings at the last ember in the gray ashes.

The bird fluttered and flapped, trying to bring the ember back to life. The bird moved closer to the ember, waving air at it. The bird stood right over the ember and flapped his wings as fast as he could.

And gradually, as the bird fanned the air at the ashes, the ember turned from dull red to bright orange. The bird flapped and flapped, and the ember flickered.

The little bird stayed there as the ember got hotter and hotter, his wings flapping and flapping until the ember burst back into life.

The bird staggered backward as the flames brushed his feathers.

The father and son both took deep breaths of warm air; they sighed and they rolled over.

And the polar bear realized he wasn't going to get his supper from behind the ice wall. So he limped away, his paws blackened from the fire he had tried to put out.

The little brown bird flew slowly back to his low bush on the snowy hill.

The father and son woke up safe the next morning and returned to their village, never knowing the danger they had been in nor the kindness and bravery that had saved them.

So that is why polar bears are white all over, except for the black skin on their paws.

And that is why we all know a little brown bird with a bright red breast, which is still glowing with the heat of the fire he fanned back to life.

Missing Winter
Canaanite myth,
Eastern Mediterranean

When gods fight among themselves, the winners rule the earth.

So when Baal, the god of rain, lightning, wind, and snow, defeated Yam, the prince of the sea, he felt like the strongest god in the world. Baal demanded that El, the oldest god, grant him the right to build a palace.

El agreed, but only after the warrior goddess Anat threatened to make El's gray

beard run with blood if he didn't honor her brother, Baal.

Baal built a palace on an ice-capped mountain, where cool winds could blow through the windows and where he could command the rain, snow, thunder, and lightning.

When the palace was finished, Baal decided to hold a feast to show off his power. He arranged for a year's worth of bread and wine to be brought to his palace, then he invited Anat and he invited El, his wife, Athirat, and their son, Athtar.

But the guest list looked too short. Baal wanted more gods to come and bow down to him in his own home.

So he sent an invitation to Mot, the god of death, who ruled the underworld and also ruled the sun.

Mot responded with an invitation of his own: "How dare you invite me to a feast of

bread and wine? I am not an ox or a stag; I am a lion in the desert, so I hunger for flesh and I thirst for blood. Yet you insult me by offering me bread and wine. So now the flesh and blood I yearn for is your flesh and your blood, Baal. I demand that you come to my land and feast at my table. If you do not attend, then I will send my servants to drag you down."

When he heard this message, Baal shivered. He'd beaten a sea monster and built a palace but that didn't make him the most powerful god after all.

So Baal canceled the feast and left his palace by the back door. He found a dead calf in a field, dressed the calf in his robes, and enchanted it to look like a god, hoping Mot would be fooled.

But when Mot's servants took the calf to his feasting table, Mot chewed on its legs and spluttered in disgust. "This is not the flesh of a god, this is the flesh of a beast. Bring me Baal!"

So Baal hid from Mot's servants.

He hid in his boat of snow-clouds. But the servants of death found him. He hid in the rocks at the end of the sun's journey in the west. But the servants of death found him. He hid in the ruined palace of Yam, his old enemy. But the servants of death found him.

Eventually Baal realized that no one can hide from death forever and that hiding in corners would not look good in the legend of his life.

So Baal stood, dressed himself splendidly in lightning and snow, and walked down to the underworld.

Baal said to Mot, "How kind of you to invite me to your home." He sat at Mot's table and he smiled as Mot offered him a dish of mud. Baal knew mud was the food of the dead.

Then, like a polite guest, Baal ate the food in front of him. After three mouthfuls, he choked on it and fell to the filthy floor of Mot's throne room.

When Mot stopped laughing, he ordered the sun to shine longer and brighter and hotter.

Without Baal in his palace, there was no one to bring cooling winds or soothing rain. So the land suffered under the harsh summer. The earth was dry and dusty; the sky was burning thin.

The gods mourned Baal and hoped that someone else could take his place, someone who could be winter and bring life back to the earth. But when El's son Athtar sat in Baal's throne, his feet didn't reach the ground. No one but Baal could end the drought and famine of Mot's summer.

So Anat dressed for battle. With the severed heads of death's servants hanging from her shoulders and their severed hands hanging from her belt, she marched through the underworld to find her brother.

When she arrived in the throne room, she didn't draw her sword. Instead she spoke politely. "Mot, lord of death, please return Baal to life and the world."

Mot sniggered. "Aw, poor little Anat, are you missing your brother? You can come and join Baal here at my table. Oh no, there he is *under* my table. Baal is dead, and that's how he'll stay."

Anat kept her fingers away from her sword and spoke calmly once more. "Without Baal, the world above is dying. The summer is endless, the ground is hard, people cannot plant crops. If you don't return Baal to us, all the people will die."

"I eat the dead," answered Mot. "The endless summer pleases me and I am hungry for the death it will bring. So I will not return Baal and I will command the sun to shine forever."

"But Mot, if all the people die in this one summer, you will have a full belly now, then be starving forever. Is a world with no life really what you want?"

Mot grinned. "When did you turn soft, Anat? When did you care about little people's lives? I have watched you reduce whole cities to puddles of blood. Come and join me; come and dine on death with me. And as we feast, I will tell you how your brother died. Baal died shivering and hiding, sneaking and cheating, then choking and gagging. He did not die like a god. He died like a . . . rat!"

Anat screamed, drew her sword, and leaped at Mot.

Mot stood, raised his arms, and called on his powers. But his main weapon was fear, and Anat did not recognize fear. Mot was used to ruling the dead, and the dead don't usually fight back, so within moments Anat had knocked him down to the floor of his own throne room.

Once Mot was on the floor, Anat plowed lines in his flesh with her sword. She sliced him into tiny grains, then ground him into flour under her heels. She took handfuls of Mot to the dry fields and scattered him far and wide, screaming all the time that he must give back her brother.

When she returned to Mot's throne room to stir his blood into the mud, she heard Baal spluttering and choking. Anat slapped him hard on the back and Baal spat up the mud caught in his throat, then he took a deep breath and crawled out from under death's table.

So Anat returned Baal to life. Baal ended the endless summer with cool rain in the valleys and cold snow on the mountains. And crops grew again.

But over the months of winter all the tiny ground-up particles of Mot, hidden deep in the earth, crawled toward each other and clung together. So the next year Mot rose from the depths and attacked Baal again.

Now, every year, Anat has to rescue her brother Baal from the hot grasp of the god of death to allow the cool winds of winter to bring life to the earth. But Anat can never grind Mot up small enough to stop him coming back next summer.

The Fox's Footprints
Cree Folktale, Canada

O nce, in the land near the top of the world, a little girl fell suddenly ill, coughing and struggling to breathe.

Her father and mother were afraid she would die, so as she lay wrapped in blankets by the fire, they asked the shaman, the wise man of their people, to help her.

The shaman felt the little girl's forehead and held her hand. He listened to her coughing and he listened to the rasping sounds in her

chest. "I hear footsteps crunching on snow. I hear feet breaking through the crust of the snow."

The mother looked out of the door flap. "There's no one there."

The shaman smiled. "The footsteps are not here in the village. They are crunching through snow in her chest."

He listened again. "I hear small, light feet, struggling through the deep snow and the sharp crust. It's a little silver fox."

He listened one more time. "As the fox moves away across the snow, your daughter's spirit moves further from her body. We must track the fox and bring her to your daughter. If we do not, your daughter will die."

"I will go after the fox," said the girl's father.

"No," said the shaman. "I will go."

"But we need you here with our daughter," said her mother.

"I will stay and I will go," said the shaman.

So the shaman's body sat by the little girl, holding her hand. And the shaman's spirit went walking.

The shaman tracked the silver fox across the snow. He found her tiny, neat footprints and he followed them. But as the shaman moved across the snow, he left no footprints.

He followed the fox for miles. When he reached a sheltered spot where the fox had stopped and rested, he stopped and rested too. He lit a fire, sparks drifting up to the stars.

As the shaman's spirit sat by the fire, the shaman's body warmed up. His hand grew warmer. He gripped the little girl's fingers and she started to burn with a fever.

"She is getting worse!" called the father.

"Shhh," said the mother. "Sometimes worse comes before better . . ."

Miles away, the shaman's spirit put out the fire.

The girl cooled down.

The shaman followed the fox again.

He moved faster and the fox knew he was coming, so the fox began to run.

The fox's heart beat faster and faster with fear and exertion. The little girl's pulse got faster and faster and weaker and

weaker. The mother and father held each other tight.

The shaman's spirit caught up with the fox. He stood in front of her, blocking her way. His spirit danced around the fox, trapping her in a circle so she couldn't escape. He spoke softly to her, he calmed her down, then he pointed in the direction of the little girl's lodge. He broke the circle and the fox ran in long, skimming strides across the snow.

The shaman's spirit smiled and started the journey back.

The mother and father watched the stillness of the wise man's body and the pale face of their barely breathing daughter. Then a corner of the door flap was pushed aside and a little silver shape slid in.

The fox.

The fox trotted past the shaman's body and curled up on the blankets beside the little girl. The little girl sighed and rolled over. Her breathing

became stronger, her color came back, and she stopped coughing.

The shaman stood, his body and spirit reunited. "She is whole now. Feed and care for the fox as well as the child, and they will both thrive."

He left the family together. As he walked away, he made deep firm footprints in the snow.

Ukko and the Bear

Lapp legend, Finland

One cold, sunny morning in the north of Finland, an old man stood on the bank of a fast-running river in the middle of a forest.

The river was bouncing with joy because winter was ending, the snows were melting, and the water was running away to the sea.

The old man was bent and gray, and he looked sadly at the far bank of the river.

"The river is too fast and deep for me to cross," he said as a reindeer trotted past him.

The reindeer said, "Don't look at me, old man. I'm not going to help you across. I'm hungry and weak after the winter, and I'm off to find new spring grass to eat."

The reindeer trotted away, leaving the old man on the riverbank.

The old man stepped nearer to the edge of the foaming river.

A brown bear called from the trees, "Don't step into the river, old man! It will sweep you away! I will take you across."

The old man said, "But aren't you also hungry and weak after the winter?"

The bear nodded. "There is very little to eat in the winter, so it's a hard time for us all. I'm no more than fur and bones just now but I'm still bigger than you, and perhaps together our weight will get you safely across the river."

The man clambered onto the bear's back, feeling the bear's sharp ribs through his soft fur, and the bear stepped into the river.

The water was heavy and fast, so the bear was pushed two steps downstream for every step he took toward the opposite bank. But he struggled forward, forcing his legs and chest through the water.

Eventually the bear reached the other side and pulled himself out of the river. The old man jumped off the bear's back. The bear collapsed onto the ground, wet, gasping, and trembling.

Then the old man straightened his spine, his gray hair glowed gold, and he stood tall and magnificent.

The god Ukko, in his true form.

The god said to the bear, "Thank you for your strength, your courage, and your kindness. In return, I shall give you a gift. You will not starve through another cold winter. Instead you will fall asleep, fat and happy, in the autumn, then wake again to the plenty of spring."

The bear smiled and went off to search for his breakfast. And Ukko walked straight and tall through the cold spring sunshine.

So that is why bears sleep every winter, while reindeer work hard, pulling sleighs through the snow.

The Last Sun
Chinese myth

Long ago, when the world was new and the sky was new too, there were ten suns. Ten beautiful suns, each glowing a different color: red and blue and purple and silver and pink and orange and lilac and green and yellow and gold.

The ten suns danced in the air, making the sky above the new land of China gloriously bright. But the heat of ten suns made the earth below too hot. Too hot for rain to

fall, too hot for plants to grow, too hot for people to work.

So the great warrior Houyi decided to save the plants and the people of China by dealing with the enemy who was creating all this heat.

"I shall save us all by shooting down the suns!"

Houyi lifted his bow made of dragon tendon and his arrows made of tiger bone and he aimed at the suns.

He fired his first arrow.

And the red sun burst. As the arrow pierced the center of the sun, it exploded into thousands of sharp red sparks. It was sudden and loud and spectacular, like the first firework.

The people below cheered. But Houyi didn't stop. He pulled another arrow from his quiver and shot the next sun. Blue sparks exploded across the sky.

As he fired more arrows, the sky was lit up like a celebration by purple, silver, and pink sparks. The people were singing and dancing, but the remaining suns were terrified. They

rushed about the sky, trying to escape from the arrows.

Houyi was a wonderful archer so the points of his arrows followed the suns, anticipating their panicked circles in the sky. He shot them down one by one in a whirl of orange sparks, lilac sparks, green sparks, and yellow sparks.

As he reached for his final arrow, the last sun, wailing in fear, dived out of the sky toward Earth and hid in a cave.

As Houyi strode off to search for his prey, the people hugged and laughed.

Now there were no suns in the sky. At first the dark and the cold were a relief. The earth wasn't baked dry; the people weren't hot and tired. Everyone welcomed the very first winter.

But soon people started to shiver and the plants, which hadn't grown without water, now couldn't grow without light.

The darkness and the cold lasted for so long that the people stopped celebrating and

started to fear the dark and the cold. The first winter made them miserable.

So the people called to Houyi, "If you find the last sun, don't shoot it; ask it to return to the sky!"

Houyi tracked the last sun to a cave with a rock covering its entrance, and he asked the sun to come out.

But the sun recognized Houyi's voice and knew this man had killed all his sisters and brothers, so the sun wouldn't come out.

Then all the people of China asked the sun politely to shine again. But the sun had heard those people cheer and laugh as the other suns burst and died. So the sun didn't leave the cave.

All the animals wanted winter to end, so they also asked the sun to return to the sky.

The tiger roared a demand for the sun to come out. But the roar just frightened the sun further to the back of the cave.

The cow mooed a plea for the sun to come out. But the deep, lowing moo was so sad that the sun hid even deeper in the earth.

Then the cockerel stood on top of a small hill and crowed. He didn't ask the last sun for anything, he just raised his sharp head and sang.

"Cock a doodle doo!"

The last sun wondered who was so happy.

"Cock a doodle doo!"

The sun crept to the entrance of the cave.

"Cock a doodle doo!"

And the sun saw the bright little cockerel singing a bright loud song.

"Cock a doodle doo!"

The last sun decided that there was still hope and happiness in the world after all. The sun bowed to the cockerel and the cockerel bowed to the sun. Then the last sun returned to the sky to shine down every day.

The sun gave the cockerel a gift of a red crown. And in return the cockerel sings every morning to welcome the sun with a cheerful song and to make sure the sun never leaves Earth to suffer such a long, dark, cold winter ever again.

Blind Winter
Viking myth

The Viking gods were a rowdy family, always fighting, feasting, arguing, and heading out of Asgard to challenge giants to battle whenever they got bored. But the Viking gods all agreed on one thing: their fondness for Baldur.

Baldur was the Viking sun god. He was the god of summer and light and warmth. He had curly red hair, a big bright smile, and a huge loud laugh, so he lit up every room he walked into.

Baldur was the Viking gods' favorite god.

But one night Baldur's mother Frigga dreamed that Baldur was going to die. That would be a distressing dream for any mother, but when a god or goddess dreams, it's a glimpse of the future. Gods' dreams come true.

So Frigga asked Odin, the chief of the Viking gods, for permission to try to protect Baldur, to try to change the future.

"I know it's not easy to divert a dream," she said, "but surely no one wants Baldur to die?"

And no one did. When Odin consulted the gods they agreed that the god of summer was so important, so bright and warm and cheerful, that it was worth trying to prevent the dream coming true.

So Frigga crossed the rainbow bridge from Asgard to Earth and she asked everything she could think of to promise not to harm Baldur.

She asked fire to promise; she asked water and earth and stone to promise, and they all promised not to harm Baldur.

She asked wind and metal and disease and they promised too. She asked the birds of the air, the fish in the sea, the animals in the field, and the plants with their roots in the ground. She asked them all to promise not to harm Baldur. They all loved the sun god and they all loved summer, so they all promised.

Frigga returned to Asgard and announced, "I've done it! Baldur is safe!" She listed everything she had asked not to harm her son, everything that had promised, and the gods agreed that Baldur was now definitely safe.

Because they were Viking gods and because Baldur's safety was a great excuse for a celebration, they feasted!

During the feast, Loki, the Viking trickster god, saw a chance for a little bit of mischief.

"I have an idea," he called out at the end of a song about counting giants' toes. "I have an idea for a game! If nothing can harm Baldur, then we can throw anything we like at him and it won't hurt him."

This sounded like an excellent idea to the Viking gods. So Baldur stood at the far end

of the hall and the other gods threw things at him.

Thor threw a soup ladle at Baldur.

It bounced off and Baldur laughed.

Freya threw a stool at Baldur.

It bounced off and Baldur laughed again.

Tir threw a shield at Baldur.

It bounced off too, and Baldur laughed his great loud warm laugh.

The Viking gods thought this was a *great* game. So the next time they had a feast, they played it again. They brought the strangest things they could find to throw at the sun god:

Small boats.

Large sheep.

Sharp hats.

Garden sheds.

They awarded themselves points for hitting different bits of Baldur: on his knees, his tummy, his chest, his nose . . .

They even had a name for the game: Let's Chuck Stuff At Baldur!

It became the most popular way to end a feast, with lots of shouting and that great, big, warm smile and great, big, loud laugh from Baldur as another spear or frying pan or table bounced off without harming him.

But Loki noticed that one of the gods never joined in the game, and Loki saw a chance for a bit more mischief, or perhaps something more than mischief.

The god who wasn't joining in was Baldur's brother. Baldur was god of summer, sun, and light, so his twin Hodur was god of winter, cold, and darkness. And Hodur was blind.

As the god of winter sat in his dark corner, surrounded by flurries of snow and with ice creeping up the legs of his stool, Loki sidled up to Hodur and asked, "Don't you want to join in?"

"I would love to join in but I can't. I can't see to choose something to throw and I can't see to aim at Baldur. So I can't join in."

Loki leaned in close to Hodur's ear and said in his most charming, most persuasive voice, "Would you like me to help you?"

Hodur said, "Yes please, that would be very kind."

Loki smiled and left Asgard.

He crossed the rainbow bridge to Earth and began searching for something that Hodur could throw.

Loki had been listening when Frigga listed everything that had promised not to harm Baldur and his quick trickster's mind had noticed one little gap. So he searched for a forest, then he searched through the forest for an oak tree, then on the oak tree he searched for mistletoe, with its plain green leaves and bright white berries.

He was searching for mistletoe because mistletoe is a parasite. Mistletoe doesn't get its goodness from the earth, it sucks the goodness out of the tree it grows on. So mistletoe doesn't have its roots in the ground. And Frigga hadn't asked mistletoe to promise not to harm Baldur.

So when Loki found what he was looking for, he broke off one sprig of mistletoe and sharpened it into a dart. Then he returned to the feasting hall in Asgard, where the gods were still throwing boots and hammers at the god of summer.

Loki walked up to the god of winter and whispered, "Do you still want to play?"

"Yes please."

"Then hold out your hand."

Loki put the dart in Hodur's hand, Loki closed Hodur's cold fingers around the dart, Loki lifted Hodur's arm and aimed it at Baldur's chest.

Then Loki stepped back into the shadows.

Loki said softly, "Throw it."

Hodur threw the dart of mistletoe straight at his brother's chest.

The mistletoe, which had promised nothing, flew through the air. The mistletoe hit Baldur's chest, pierced his skin, and drove right into his heart.

Baldur, beloved god of summer, fell down dead.

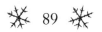

And Baldur stayed dead. The Viking gods, with their games and tricks, were closer in nature to fragile humans than to the immortal gods of warmer lands. So when Baldur died, he stayed dead.

Summer died, and summer did not come back to life. Summer did not return.

The Viking gods were horrified at their sudden loss and they had no idea who was responsible.

Was it Frigga, for forgetting to ask mistletoe to promise?

Was it Hodur, for throwing a dart at his own brother's heart?

Or was it possibly someone else?

Loki moved further back into the shadows, wondering if the blind god knew who had put the mistletoe, the weapon of winter, into his hand.

Then he heard Hodur tell the others, "I didn't choose the weapon but I know who did. I recognized his voice. Loki offered to help me play. Loki put the dart in my hand. Loki told me to throw it."

Loki had already left the hall but now the Viking gods knew who had tricked winter into killing summer.

The Viking gods hunted Loki down and eventually they caught him in a net of his own making. But the terrible revenge they took on Loki started a new story rolling, a story which led to the battle of Ragnarok and caused the end of the Viking gods' world.

Five White Eagles
Venezuelan legend

C aribay was the daughter of the chief of the Mirripuyes people, but people said that she must really be the daughter of the sun and the moon. How else could anyone explain the brilliance of her eyes, the gleam on her skin, and the shine in her long, black hair? She seemed to be made of light.

Caribay knew she was beautiful. Every day she dressed to show off her beauty. She wore

beads on her clothes, bone collars around her neck, and flowers in her hair, all to make herself more beautiful than anyone else of the mountain people.

One day she was at the riverbank searching for shiny pebbles to sew onto her poncho, when she saw five white eagles fly overhead.

She had never seen anything more beautiful, not even her own reflection in the water. The eagles were so elegant and their feathers gleamed so perfectly white.

Caribay was jealous of their beauty. "If I had those white feathers in my hair, then I would be even more beautiful than the sun and the moon."

She followed the eagles as they flew higher into the mountains. She tracked their shadows on the ground, hoping the birds would grow tired of flying before she grew tired of following.

The five white eagles flew higher and higher. Caribay was a fast runner and a nimble climber, so she kept pace with them for hours, but eventually she began to tire.

So she shouted, "Oh sun in the sky, I am told that my beauty echoes yours. Help me trap these eagles so I can pluck their feathers and become as beautiful as you."

The sun watched the girl chasing the eagles, then he sank below the horizon so she could no longer see their shadows.

Caribay sighed and continued to follow the eagles in the dusk, tracking their pale gleam in the darkening sky and the sound of their occasional wingbeats in the air.

And she yelled, "Oh moon in the sky, I am told my beauty echoes yours. Help me trap these eagles so I can pluck their feathers and become as beautiful as you."

The moon looked down and saw that the eagles were tired of being chased by the girl shrieking behind them. So the moon threw down her rays to touch the eagles.

The five eagles settled on the five highest peaks in the Sierra de Merida. The eagles stayed still, their white feathers edged by moonlight, as Caribay scrambled toward them.

"Well done, moon, at least you're more use to your beautiful daughter than the sun," she gasped, and she reached up to yank out the first eagle's tail feathers.

When she touched the eagle's tail, she screamed because it was not soft and warm like feathers should be. The eagle felt solid and cold.

The moon had changed the eagles into the icy peaks of the mountains.

The eagle turned around slowly to look at Caribay, its beak sharp and hard as a blade, its eyes shining with the chilly light of the moon.

Caribay screamed again and ran down the mountain. "I don't want the white feathers any more," she shrieked. "Just let me go home." But she couldn't find her way home. She ran around the mountains, lost in the dark, screaming and shrieking.

As she ran and shrieked, the eagles shook themselves and settled more comfortably.

When they moved, their smallest feathers fell, whirling cold and white through the air.

Those feathers were the very first snowflakes.

Caribay never found her way out of the mountain tops. As she ran and shrieked, she became the spirit of the wind. So now, Caribay is often heard but never seen, which is very frustrating for a girl who loved to show off her beauty.

The white eagles still live happily on the tops of the five highest mountains. All year round, the eagles can be seen as five gleaming white peaks.

And in the winter, when the storms rage around the mountains and they hear the shrieks of Caribay trying to find her way home, the five eagles shake and settle. Then their white, feathery snowflakes fall, covering all the lower mountains in the Andes.

And people agree that the mountains and the snowflakes are far more beautiful than Caribay ever was.

The Hero with
Hairy Trousers

Norse legend

Almost nine hundred years ago, a shipload of Vikings sheltered from a snowstorm in a stone-age tomb called Maes Howe in Orkney. As they waited, surrounded by ancient bones, rather than telling ghost stories, they carved graffiti on the walls. Among the runes about beautiful women and hidden treasure, one of the carvings is about a Viking hero called Ragnar Lodbrok.

Ragnar Lodbrok sounds like a very heroic name until you realize that Lodbrok means "hairy trousers." There really was a Viking hero called Ragnar Hairy Trousers. And this is how he got his name . . .

Long ago, a Viking king was riding through a forest when he saw something glitter. Vikings love treasure, especially other people's treasure, so he jumped down from his horse. But the glitter wasn't coins or jewels—it was an animal. A little shiny animal with sharp golden scales, big purple eyes, tiny fluttering wings, and a long snaky tail. And when it sneezed, it sneezed sparks.

It was a baby dragon.

It was a very cute baby dragon. So the Viking king picked it up, balanced it on the front of his saddle, and took it home to his castle as a gift for his daughter, Thora.

Thora was delighted with her pet dragon. She cuddled it and stroked it and fed it herself every morning.

At first, because the dragon only had tiny teeth and little jaws, she fed the dragon

ripped-up raw rabbit. (Thora was a Viking princess and she didn't mind a bit of blood on her hands.)

Soon the dragon was bigger and Thora didn't have to rip up the rabbit. She just threw whole rabbits into the air for the dragon to catch and eat.

When rabbit wasn't enough to fill the dragon's growing belly, Thora started to feed the dragon chopped-up raw sheep. (Thora was a Viking princess and she was quite handy with an ax.)

Soon the dragon was so huge that Thora didn't need to chop up the sheep. All she had to do was peel off the sheepskin every morning. (Dragons don't like getting wool caught between their teeth.)

When sheep weren't filling the dragon's belly either, Thora decided it was time to go to market and buy a herd of cows.

But on the day she left the castle to buy the cows, no one else was brave enough to feed the dragon breakfast. So the hungry dragon ate one of the castle gardeners.

The king wasn't pleased. He decided to banish the dragon to the far northern wastes. He raised his arm, he pointed to the northern wastes, and he shouted at the dragon.

But dragons don't usually do what they're told, and this dragon didn't want to go to the far northern wastes because there wasn't enough food there. So the dragon flew to the top of the highest mountain in the land and made a lair.

Then the dragon swooped down every day to grab farmers from the fields or fishermen from the fjords and take them up to his lair to eat them.

Soon no one wanted to farm or to fish for fear of being eaten by the dragon.

Eventually, with his people hungry and afraid, the king sent out a proclamation: "Anyone who can rid us of this dragon will win half the kingdom and the right to ask Princess Thora for her hand in marriage."

Half a kingdom is a prize worth having and Thora, when she washed her hands, was a lovely princess. So lots of heroes arrived at

the castle, all equipped with horses, armor, and lances.

They rode one by one to the mountain, left their horses at the foot, and climbed up with their shiny, metal armor and their long, sharp lances.

When the first hero climbed to the top, the dragon saw him coming. The dragon opened his huge jaws and the dragon breathed fire . . .

Inside his fancy, shiny, metal armor, the hero baked like bread in a bread tin. And when the hero was all nice and crunchy, the dragon ate him.

So the next hero started to climb up the mountain with his shiny, metal armor and his long, sharp lance. The dragon saw him coming and the dragon breathed fire . . .

Inside his heavy, metal armor, the hero roasted like a parsnip in a roasting tin. And when the hero was caramelized and soft in the middle, the dragon ate him.

After a few more baked, roasted, grilled, and fried heroes, suddenly there weren't so many heroes keen to climb the mountain. In

fact, there was now only one person left who was prepared to climb the mountain and take on the dragon.

His name was Ragnar and he wasn't a hero or a prince or a warrior. He was a kitchen boy in the king's castle. But he had liked Thora for a long time and he wanted the chance to ask her to be his wife.

Ragnar didn't have a horse or a lance or any armor. All he had was a key to the kitchen.

So one winter evening, he crept into the kitchen and he found a broom handle, some string, and a carving knife. Then he crept up to Thora's chambers and he asked her for three of the sheepskins she had peeled from the dragon's breakfasts. Thora gave Ragnar the best sheepskins she had, and she gave him a smile too.

Then Ragnar walked through the long winter night, all the way to the mountain, and he climbed the mountain in the dark. When he was near the summit, he sat down by a mountain stream and he started to cut the sheepskin with the knife.

He cut himself a pair of trousers, a jacket, and a big hat with flaps. He pulled the clothes on, woolly side out, so he was wearing fleecy, fluffy sheepskin all over.

He tied the knife to the end of the broom handle to make a spear, and he put the spear down by the side of the stream.

Next, Ragnar lay down in the stream, with only his nose poking out, and he stayed in the water until the fleece was soaking wet.

Then he climbed out, picked up the spear, and stood very still by the stream.

And as his breath froze in front of him in the cold winter air, so the water in the fleece froze too.

Ragnar had made himself armor of ice.

As the sun rose, he climbed to the summit of the mountain.

In the light of the sunrise, the dragon saw him coming and the dragon breathed fire.

But Ragnar's armor of ice kept him cool as he walked toward the dragon.

So the dragon breathed fire again. Hotter, redder fire.

And Ragnar's armor steamed a little but inside the icy fleece, he stayed cool.

The dragon breathed fire again. His hottest, reddest, fiercest fire.

And clouds of steam billowed off the armor of ice as Ragnar walked forward. But inside the armor of ice, Ragnar stayed cool.

The clouds of steam blinded the dragon, and while it couldn't see, Ragnar took one last step forward and drove his spear into the dragon's heart.

The dragon fell down dead.

Ragnar used the knife to cut off the dragon's head.

Then he walked back to the castle carrying the head to prove he had killed the dragon. But as he walked back, the rising sun warmed the air, and Ragnar's icy armor finally melted. So he was squelching at every step by the time he reached the castle.

When he walked into the Great Hall, with the dragon's head dripping blood and his sheepskin armor dripping water, he won himself a new Viking hero name.

Ragnar Lodbrok, Ragnar Hairy Trousers.

He also won half the kingdom and the right to ask Thora to marry him. Thora must have forgiven him for killing her pet dragon because she smiled and said yes.

Ragnar and Thora lived happily ever after and had lots of children. And when those children asked for pets of their own, Ragnar and Thora didn't give them baby dragons. They gave them puppies instead.

Where I found these Winter's Tales

I didn't invent these Winter's Tales—each of these stories has been told somewhere in the world for a very long time. But I do change stories as I tell them so they make sense in my head and sound real in my voice. The stories in this collection are the versions I tell out loud, rather than exact copies of the stories that inspired me. If you share these stories, please feel free to change them too, and make them into your stories!

When I retell stories in books, I like to let readers know where I found the versions that inspired me so you can go back and find out more about them yourself, and also because every storyteller owes a nod of thanks to the storyteller or writer who first showed them the way into a story . . .

The Seeds of Winter
Greek myth

This is probably the best known myth about the seasons, and I've known Persephone's story since I was a child, so I have no idea where I first read it. However, the best version I ever heard, which inspired my own adaptation, was told by a very talented first year pupil at Denny High School near Falkirk. So thanks for the flowers, Sam Edgar!

The Snow Bear and the Trolls
Norwegian Folktale

I first found this story in *Scandinavian
Stories* by Margaret Sperry (published by JM
Dent, 1971) and loved it immediately. I still
changed it as I told it, though. My snow bear
doesn't talk, for example, and my trolls might
be a bit smellier . . .

The Prince of Wolves
Tsimshian Folktale, Canada

I found this story a few years ago while researching a novel about shape-changing wolves in a Scottish forest. It's from a collection called *Wolf Tales: Native American Children's Stories*, edited by Mary Powell (Ancient City Press, 1992) and I've always liked it because it helps to balance all those big, bad wolf stories out there!

The Ibis Brings Spring
Yamana myth, Tierra del Fuego

This is a combined adaptation of two short myths from *Folk Literature of the Yamana Indians*, edited by Johannes Wilbert (University of California Press, 1977). I was delighted to find these winter stories told by the people who live nearer than anyone else to the Antarctic and the South Pole.

The Hag of Winter
Scottish myth

I have heard and read dozens of different versions of this ancient Celtic story about the Cailleach (which is Gaelic for old woman) so the version I tell is a patchwork of many others. I must admit that I've changed this story more than usual—I was always a bit annoyed by Brid just waiting for Angus to save her, so I came up with a way for her to signal Angus and also let her fight the storm hags. If you want to read a very traditional version, try *Wonder Tales from Scottish Myth and Legend*, by Donald Alexander McKenzie (Black and Sons, 1917).

The Spiders' Christmas
Ukrainian Folktale

I first met these cheerful little spiders in the *Lion Storyteller Christmas Book* by Bob Hartmann (Lion Publishing, 2000) and was delighted to discover, after a little research, the Ukrainian (and German) tradition of spider decorations on Christmas trees.

Ice and Fire
Maori myth, New Zealand

This is the only story I tell about someone's first experience of winter weather, and I love sharing it with children because when Ngatoro is climbing the mountain, someone always whispers, "It's snow!" long before I say what the white stuff is. I first found the story in *Myths and Legends of Maoriland* by AW Reed (Allen and Unwin, 1946) and adapted it after I'd done some research into legends about the Maoris' arrival in Aotearoa.

The Hungry Polar Bear
Canadian Folktale

This was one of the first traditional tales I ever told out loud, having found a version of it by Alison Hedger in *Children's Christmas Songbook* (Chester Music, 2003) and then added details of my own. So this was my first winter story and my first bear story!

Missing Winter
Canaanite myth,
Eastern Mediterranean

After telling so many stories about people (and gods) who want winter to go away and spring or summer to return, I was fascinated by this myth showing the opposite, because in hot countries winter is the fertile time and summer is the barren time. Baal's story was discovered on ancient tablets in the ruined city of Ugarit in Syria, and translated in *Canaanite Myths and Legends* by JCL Gibson (T&T Clark, Edinburgh, 1978).

The Fox's Footprints
Cree Folktale, Canada

This is a Cree Windigo tale, which I found in Howard Norman's *Where the Chill Came From* (North Point Press, 1982). I admit that my version is simplified and somewhat altered, though I hope it retains the mystery and beauty of the tribal tale.

Ukko and the Bear
Lapp legend, Finland

I've known and told this story for years but didn't track down a written source until I saw one version of it (not exactly the one I know and tell) in *Scandinavian Stories* by Margaret Sperry (published by JM Dent, 1971). I still think it would have been easier if Ukko had just changed into a god *before* he crossed the river.

The Last Sun
Chinese myth

I first read this story in *The Return of The Light* by Carolyn McVickar Edwards (Marlowe and Company, 2000), then found a few more details in the *Handbook of Chinese Mythology* by Lihui Yang and Deming An (Oxford University Press, 2008), and added a few fireworks when I adapted it to tell myself.

Blind Winter
Viking myth

I first came across this story in Roger Lancelyn Green's wonderful *Saga of Asgard* (Penguin Books, 1960). However, because I love Viking stories, I've probably read dozens of other versions since, all of which may have contributed to my telling of this wonderful and chilling story.

Five White Eagles
Venezuelan legend

I am very grateful to my mom, who translated this story for me from the Spanish language version in *Kuai-Mare, Mitos Aborigenes de Venezuela* by Maria Manuela de Cora (Editorial Oceanida, 1957) and will probably be quite surprised when she discovers the changes I've made when I tell the story in my voice!

The Hero with Hairy Trousers
Norse legend

I searched out this story after seeing the runes about Ragnar Lodbrok at Maes Howe in Orkney. I eventually found it in one of my brother's old storybooks: *A Book of Dragons* by Roger Lancelyn Green (Hamish Hamilton 1970). It's my favorite dragon story, and I have probably told it in hundreds of schools. When I tell Ragnar's story to real children, I throw ripped up rabbits and raw sheep around the room. (Imaginary rabbits and sheep, of course, because I'm not a Viking princess . . .)